Women at the Well

A collaborative craft project storying responses to Scripture

ISBN 978-1-908860-97-2

A portion of the proceeds of this book will be donated for the promotion of water conservation around the world.

Book compiled by Henrietta Cozens; cover artwork by Sue Holbrook
'24: Made with 24 quills, to remember families in Jordan who have just 24 hours of running water a week'

With special thanks to Edi Wilson of WEC International, and
Dr Rana Abu-Mounes, Research Fellow of the Centre for Muslim-Christian Studies, Oxford, for their contributions to this project.

Introduction

In January 2021 we advertised for women in Gloucestershire to join a community craft group. We would story our responses to the themes of women at wells in the Bible and the Qur'an. Quilling, the technique we chose, involves rolling, shaping and gluing strips of paper together to create decorative designs. During the Renaissance, French and Italian nuns and monks used quilling to decorate book covers and religious items.

Using Zoom as our meeting space, we first encountered Hagar, who was cast out of her community into the desert with her young son. God miraculously provided water for her, sustaining her life. Her actions inspire many during their Mecca 'Hajj' pilgrimage today. Next, a locally-outcast Samaritan woman met a stranger at Jacob's well, who told her all she had ever done. She dropped her water jar, and rushed to tell others she had met the Messiah. Her story is retold in John 4 in the Bible. Jesus own mother, Maryam, was given by God a spring of water at her feet during childbirth, in The Chapter of Mary 19, in the Holy Qur'an. Lastly, there was a young woman waiting to collect water for her elderly father's livestock. A kind younger man, Moses, saw her need and offered to get the water for her. This well thus becomes the location where these two, who would later marry each other, first meet. The passages recounting these stories can be found in the centre of this book.

As our group of 30 women reflected on these stories of physical water sites being the places of spiritual encounter and change, we also heard how Muslims and Christians are working together in Jordan to conserve the precious gift of water. We discussed the gift and the power of water itself, and the need to conserve it and share it.

We hope that you, too, will enter into a journey of reflection, faith, hope and action, as you encounter the various stories of women at the well through our artwork.

Henrietta Cozens, Georgina Jardim, Zaheera Nanabawa

A Reflection on How our Project Came About

I know Georgina and Zaheera from The Holy Book Club, which they started five years ago as part of WINGZ, the Women's Inclusive Network Gloucestershire. When Georgina suggested running a project in 2021, to bring women together afresh around Scripture but with a creative element, I wondered if we could really do it, and also would people join?

But as I read her proposal, I felt a pleasant lightness in my spirit about it. I was already sold on the idea of reading scripture with others, (with people from one's own faith, another faith, or no faith), and thought the element of creativity and reflection would suit many of the talented women in our community. The environmental aspect of this particular project caught my attention because only a few months before I had suggested to my church leader that we join the EcoChurch scheme, and she had said she'd been praying about who to ask to lead it, and would I consider it? I could see God building a theme for this season.

We had confirmation that our artwork could be displayed at the Christian Arts Festival in Cheltenham so we successfully applied for some funding to cover craft materials from a Christian charity which was delighted to support the project. We gathered our team, and put an advert together. Still, would anyone actually want to come? We settled on going ahead if we had 12 people including ourselves. The first day we released that advert, 12 people signed up! I felt God's gentle confirmation and assurance to run with this.

I especially appreciated coming together as people from different backgrounds but with similar interests. The pandemic meant that screens became our communication medium. While we couldn't share food and drink and be physically together, the advantage is that we gathered people from Cheltenham, Gloucester and other places, which might well not have happened if we had all had to meet in just one city. I very much appreciated this diverse community who gave of themselves.

I also benefitted personally from dwelling on a couple of stories from Scripture longer than I would normally. Because I had to think of a quilling picture linked to what I had read, I didn't just read the passages, I often spent two weeks between our Zoom meetings thinking about each of the stories! I've learnt what meditating really means, and the benefits of working in partnership!

Henrietta Cozens
Lead Coordinator

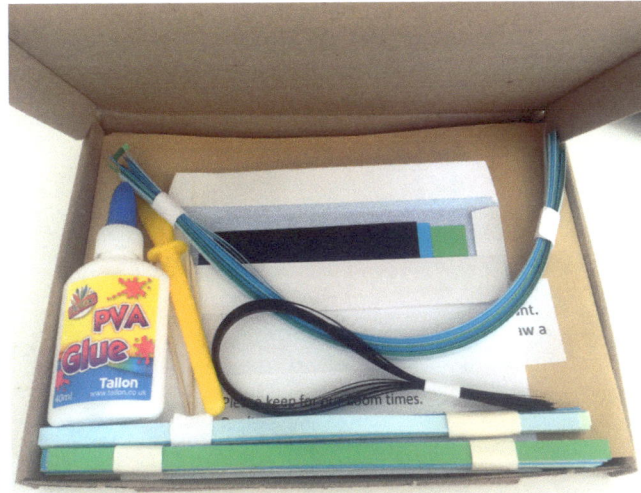

Each woman received a craft pack and was taught how to make some simple shapes using paper strips. After that, they had free choice of what to make with their resources. Six weeks later each person's panels were collected and made into one banner.

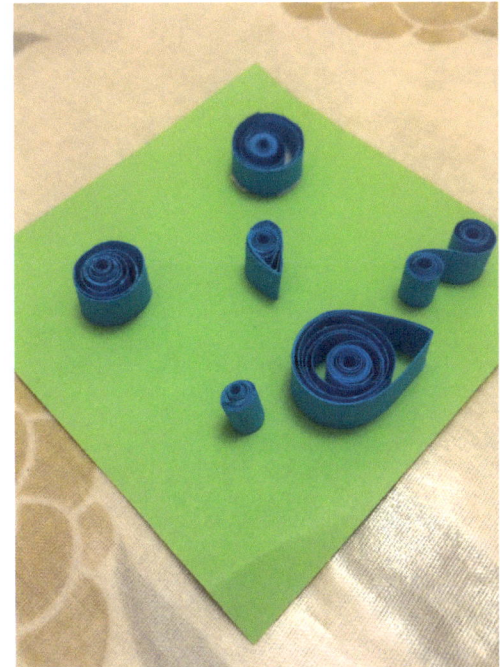

Contrasts of Hagar

I was inspired by the idea of contrasts we talked about in Hagar's life, and it also made me think about the similarities and differences between the two versions of Hagar (in the Bible) and Hajra (in the Quran)'s story.

Danielle Cooper

Sustainer

A title befitting of both water and women, sustainers of life.

Danielle Cooper

Pear

There are so many mentions of 'fruit' in the Quran - The Chapter of Abraham:

"to make the hearts of a part of the people fond of them, and provide them with fruits, so that they may give thanks".

We need water for all food, but a pear has high water content. It seems an example of that concentration, as well as having an iconic shape.

Sue Holbrook

Life Breaking Through

A simple design thinking about water and life springing up.

Danielle Cooper

Jar of Living Water

The Samaritan woman at the well (John 4) leaves behind her jar, she is so captivated by Jesus. She becomes the well herself, as she tells others about him.

Water and women seem to be an important part of Moses' history too: his mother saves him from death by putting him in a basket on the Nile river; his sister Maryam watches over him while he is on the water; and the royal princess saves him from the water. Water gives life but also has the power to destroy. These women help Moses using water to save.

Georgina Jardim

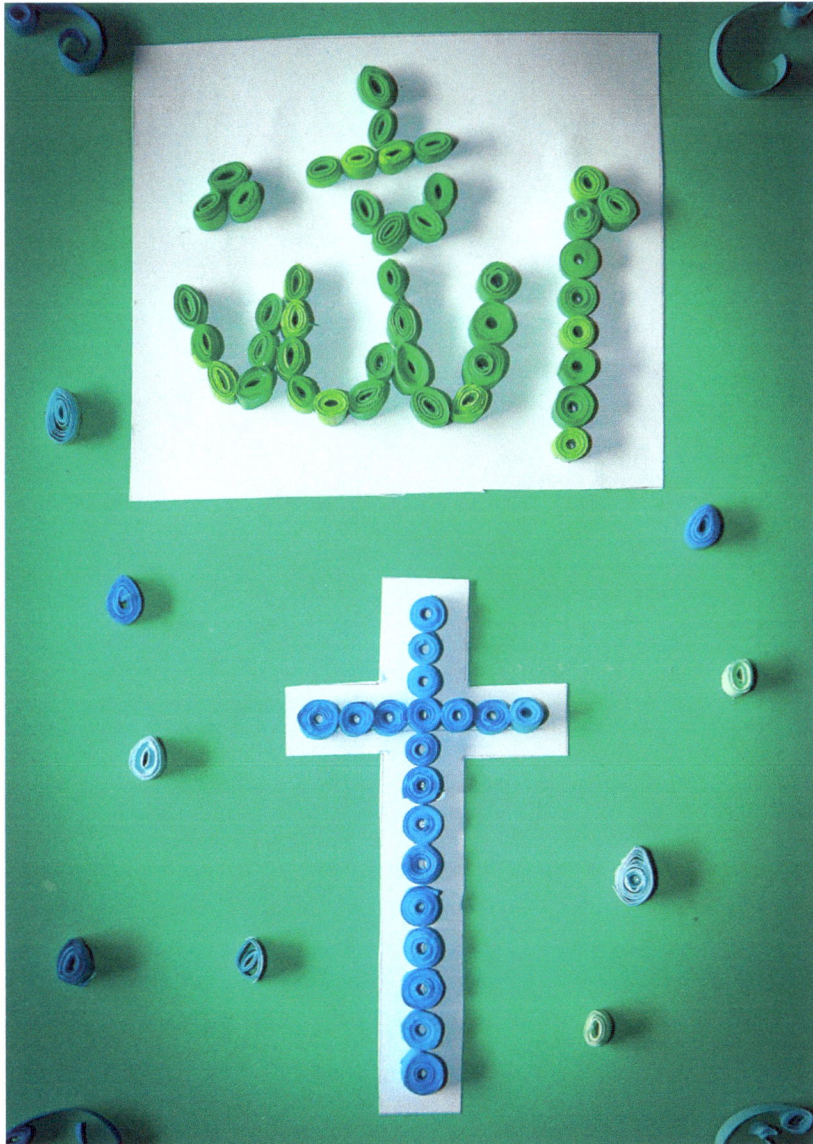

Unity

The gift of water unites us all - whatever faith (or not) that we may be.

[The word God/Allah is written in Arabic here, above the cross.]

Joan Wood

Palms

This picture of mountains in the background and date trees in the foreground shows the place where Abraham's wife went, and where she and her son received water from God.

Sherin Sheikho

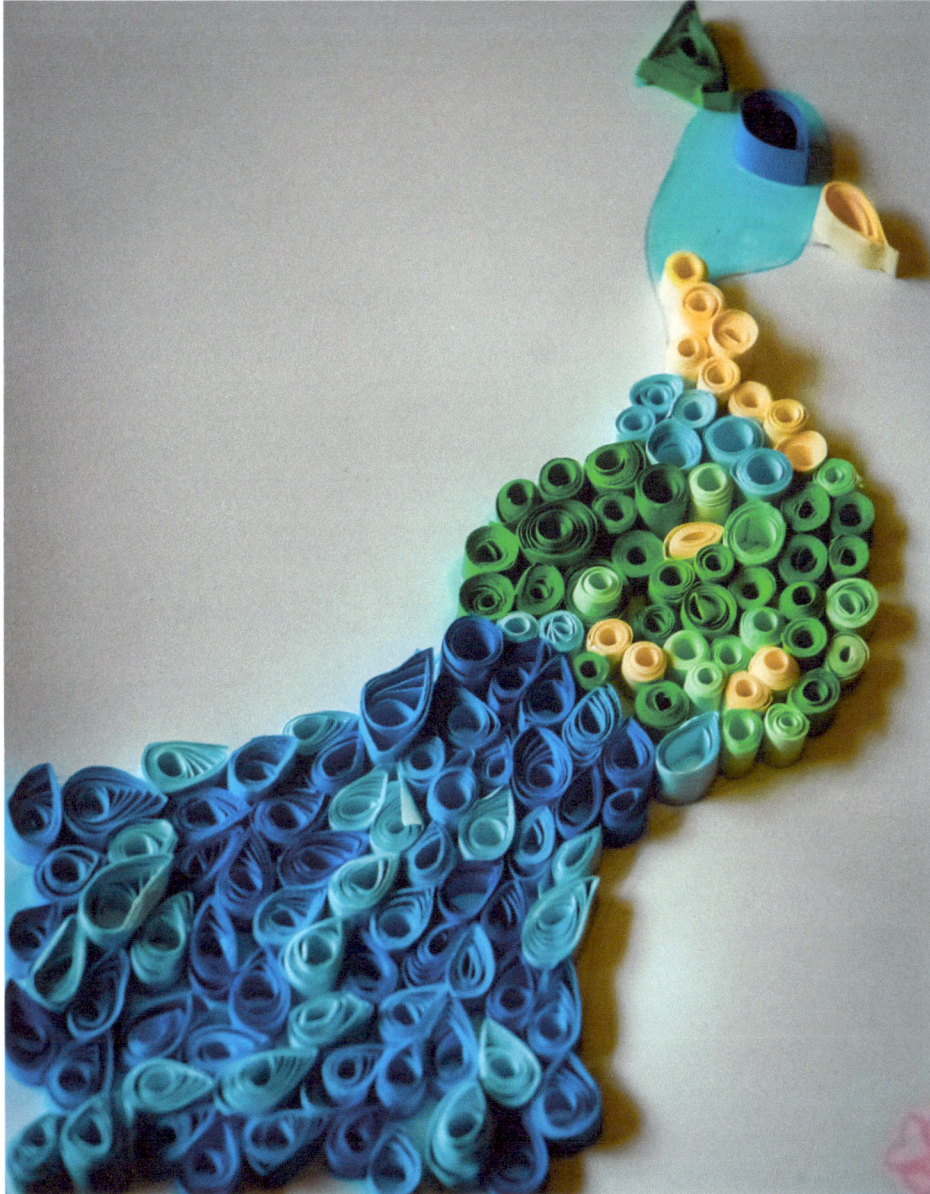

Peacock

The peacock is a symbol of eternity and paradise, a symbol of resurrection and renewal, a symbol of spring, a symbol of decoration, and the introduction of joy to souls.

Sherin Sheikho

Life

I thought about what water gives us, and
has given us through the Quran: Jonah
and the whale; Hajra at zam zam; Maryam
and the spring. Then there's the story of
the prostitute woman who gave water to a
thirsty dog in her shoe and was rewarded
with heaven in return; having that first sip
of water after you've been fasting which
is the most blessed feeling after so many
hours of not eating or drinking; the saving
of water; the not-refusing water to anyone;
the ablution and bathing, until the last
bathing of the deceased; the land, plants,
the sea, and the sky and everything in
between is so blessed by Allah because he
provides water. He provides life.

Aysha Randera

Rain, River, Tears, Waters

Our project was a really good way of discussing Scriptures, and we could explore doing this again. The focus and theme were especially apt as I am constantly thinking of water, plants and herbs, and of how much we waste and how much we use. Absorbing the true power of what water can provide as we did the petals in the craft was truly a gift! We were talking with a cousin of mine in Kolkata. He said a water pump costs 200 pounds and that would provide water for a whole community. That's less than my annual water rates here! That really hit home. On the outskirts of Kolkata in the slums they walk long distances to get clean drinking water.

Aysha Randera

Foetus Life

Child, Water, Birth, Rebirth, Life

Aysha Randera

She is Like a Tree Planted by Streams of Water

Blessed is the woman ... whose delight is in the law of God. On it she meditates day and night. She is like a tree planted by streams of water, which yields its fruit in season and whose leaf does not wither - whatever she does prospers.

[Psalm 1.2-3, Bible]

Michaela Baker

She Left Her Water Jar

Her feet fitted with the readiness that comes from the gospel of peace.

Her priorities have changed.

[This was made with 24 strips of paper, because of households in Jordan having just 24 hours of running water per week.]

Michaela Baker

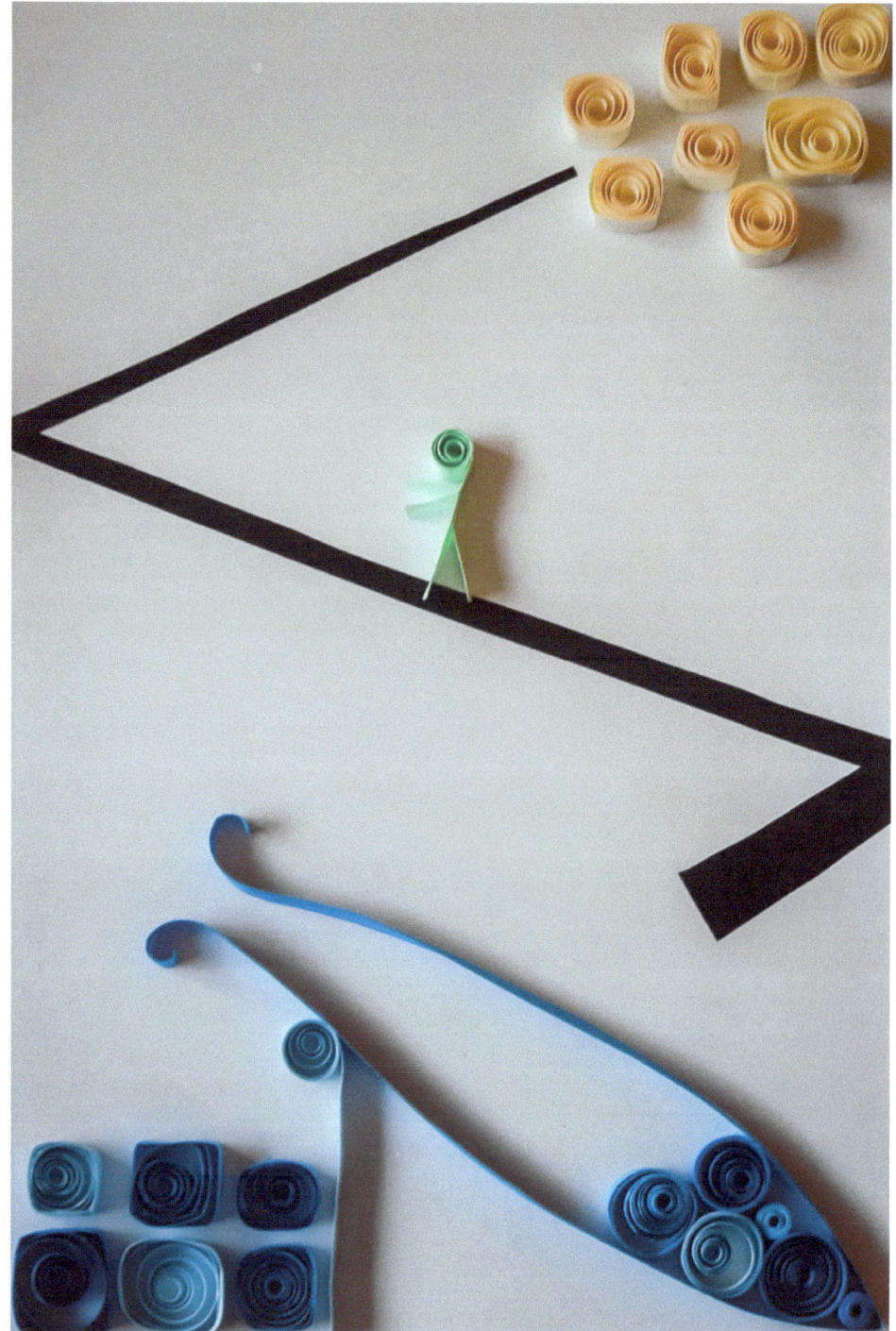

Zam-zam

The abundance of God's provision.

My cup overflows.

Hagar's experience in the wilderness.

Michaela Baker

Flourishing

Flourishing: *marked by vigorous and healthy growth*

[Merriam-Webster Dictionary]

And all the trees of the field shall know that I the Lord...have exalted the low tree ...and have made the dry tree to flourish.

[Ezekiel 17:24]

Juliet Jensen

Provision

Water runs deep beneath the mountain, which provides us with plant food and sustenance. The mountain also provides shelter and refuge.

Fatima Kholwadia

Family

I was lucky enough to travel to Jordan five
years ago, and Rana's talking [in our Zoom
meeting] took me back to dry places I'd
witnessed, and the River Jordan.

Remembering the River Jordan,
and the burning, hot, dusty day with my
daughter.
Curling paper around and glue,
and stick,
and pull.
My eldest daughter on my heart.

Sarah Rogaly

Fragile

This was created in turbulent times, with the feeling that while we spend a lot of time thinking we are in control, we can control very little indeed.

Sarah Rogaly

A Dream Catcher called 'Hope'

I found the stories we read were about hope, and trusting in God's plans.

I'm hopeful that the water crisis in Jordan and in the world improves, as water is a basic necessity of all living life, in order for survival.

Nafisa Jadwat

Crying Earth, Wasted Earth

I thought of Mother Earth crying as many of us, including myself, forget how blessed we are with water as our primary life source and how easily accessible it is to us.

This made me think more about the less fortunate that have to journey for miles by foot just to access water, no matter how unsanitary it is. A reminder that we are truly blessed and that we mustn't waste it.

Nafisa Jadwat

Tree of Life

This is the first time I tried quilling and I found it very enjoyable. I decided to quill a tree as trees give us life. I find them beautiful and majestic, and just like us they nourish and thrive with water.

Nafisa Jadwat

Springs of Living Water

God's Word gives out life-giving water; the tree rooted in it blossoms and flourishes. Hope and life can flow out again to others. Even when life seems impossible the tree is rooted and secure.

"Oh, the joys of those who…delight in doing everything God wants them to, and day and night are always meditating on his laws and thinking about ways to follow him more closely. They are like trees along a riverbank bearing luscious fruit each season without fail. Their leaves shall never wither, and all they do shall prosper."

[Psalm 1:1-3, Bible]

Edi Wilson

Life

I was thinking about the wonderful power of water: life-giving, nourishing, cleansing, renewing, refreshing and so essentially needed; but also the dangerous part of water. As I looked at my half-flooded garden, I was thinking of places like Bangladesh, where flooding causes devastation almost every year, and about the 2011 tsunami in Japan where I saw first-hand the after-effects of whole towns washed away.... the power of water. Just as water has power to restore or to devastate, the choices we make have power. I think we have daily choices, even small things to say or not say; power to heal or to wound, power to destroy or to build life.

Edi Wilson

Abundant Springs of Living Water

As we have looked at, thought about, and engaged with holy texts, I have been refreshed. God saw Hagar, Mary and the woman at the well. He saw them and he saw their real need. He offered them living water. Today he sees me. He sees my deepest need and continues to offer living water. As we created together, the group saw and heard me, giving me inspiration like springs of hope and love. We heard of countries like Jordan that face water problems. God sees; I also need to see and then speak out.

Edi Wilson

A Reflection on Our Project and Scriptures

Women at the Well has been so refreshing. Whilst being able to connect with women from a wide range of backgrounds, with faith as the central link, the learning of a new craft was ace. Following on from a discussion initially with Georgina, it was nice to know that we'd been thinking along the same lines around the importance of Hagar in the scriptures and then it was wonderful that Henrietta was able to make the ideas come alive.

It was brilliant being able to learn the skills of the quilling as a craft from Edi as the tutor, who was amazing at teaching virtually due to the restrictions of lockdown. For me, the craft had so many parallels with the subject of water. I loved that every time I made a quill and created it into a shape, the formation of the outcome was so fluid and perfect. It reminded me significantly of the Fibonacci sequence and patterns found in Allah's beautiful natural creations.

It was an honour to be able to share the story of Hagar/Hajra (Alayhiss Salaam/Peace be Upon Her) – especially the events of her running between Safa and Marwa, and the blessed presence of the angel Gabriel/Jibril (Alayhiss Salaam/Peace be Upon Them) who allowed for the nourishment and provision of the well of Zam Zam which enabled sustenance for Ismail (Alayhiss Salaam/Peace be Upon Him) and the flourishing of the settled civilisation within the blessed valley of Mecca and the sacred site of the Kaaba. It's so wonderous to me that although Hagar is not mentioned explicitly in the Quran, to this day, the sacrifices that she made and her actions are commemorated as rituals every hour to this day and will continue in the future.

The story of the Samaritan women and her engagement with Jesus (Peace be Upon Him) prompted me to think of some of the situations we are facing today where certain parts of society are being ostracised for their beliefs in spirituality. It was also a pleasure to see the bashfulness and boldness of her and reminded me of the diversity that exists within the sisterhood of Allah's female creation.

All in all, a very pleasurable project which will live on in the form of this publication, the elegant quilling creations of the women and families who have learnt the amazing craft, and the connections made between new and existing friends.

Zaheera Nanabawa
Project Director – www.wingz.org.uk

A Reflection on Our Reading of Scripture

At the end of this series of meetings, it's difficult to summarise or contain the richness of this experience! We tried new things, possibly heard new things, and we truly met each other despite being online. In coming together from different backgrounds, we created a community to learn a new craft, to think about our own texts and to think about other texts together. Reflecting on those stories from the scriptures in each other's presence was a deep experience.

But that doesn't mean it was always easy. Especially the Hagar story. Yes, it's an extraordinary story about God meeting a woman at a well but it's also difficult: the themes of mistreatment, flight and abandonment show us that life is hard. Sometimes we might even consider God's call on *our* life as hard; like God asking Abraham to sacrifice his son. Now there's a difficult story! Yet, in both Abraham and Hagar's life, we see that God provides.

I found the running between the hills, that our Muslim friends practice when they are on pilgrimage, an extraordinary demonstration of the thirst and longing for God that Hagar expressed in crying out to the Lord. Also, the story of Moses meeting his wife at the well, where once again we see a difficult life situation - the women are pushed to the side, they are mistreated, and Moses comes to their aid, himself in flight from the Pharaoh.

In the meeting at the Samaritan well, Jesus, likewise, gives the woman a place and a role within his story. Her example promises restoration: by responding to Jesus, exploring the difficult relationships and politics in her life, the Samaritan woman was restored in her community when she runs to call them to Jesus. The water he gave not only quenched her thirst but became a living well from within her.

Georgina Jardim
Project Coordinator and Scripture Leader

Qur'an, Ibrahim, The Chapter of Abraham 14:35-41

[35]When Abraham said, 'My Lord! Make this city a sanctuary and save me and my children from worshipping idols. [36]My Lord! They have indeed misled many people. So whoever follows me indeed belongs with me, and as for those who disobey me, well, You are indeed all-forgiving, all-merciful.

[37]Our Lord! I have settled part of my descendants in a barren valley, by Your sacred House, our Lord, that they may maintain the prayer. So make the hearts of a part of the people fond of them, and provide them with fruits, so that they may give thanks.

[38]Our Lord! You indeed know whatever we hide and whatever we disclose, and nothing is hidden from God on the earth or in heaven. [39]All praise belongs to God, who gave me Ishmael and Isaac despite [my] old age. My Lord indeed hears all supplications. [40]My Lord! Make me a maintainer of prayer, and my descendants [as well]. Our Lord, accept my supplication. [41]Our Lord! Forgive me, my parents, and all the faithful, on the day when the reckoning is held.

Qur'an, Al-Baqara, The Chapter of the Heifer 2:158

[158]*Safa* and *Marwah* are indeed among God's sacraments. So whoever makes *hajj* to the House, or performs the *'umrah*, there is no sin upon him to circuit between them. Should anyone do good of his own accord, then God is indeed appreciative, all-knowing.

Bible, Genesis 16:1–15

[1]Now Sarai, Abram's wife, had borne him no children. But she had an Egyptian slave named Hagar; [2]so she said to Abram, "The Lord has kept me from having children. Go, sleep with my slave; perhaps I can build a family through her." Abram agreed to what Sarai said. [3]So after Abram had been living in Canaan ten years, Sarai his wife took her Egyptian slave Hagar and gave her to her husband to be his wife. [4]He slept with Hagar, and she conceived. When she knew she was pregnant, she began to despise her mistress. [5]Then Sarai said to Abram, "You are responsible for the wrong I am suffering. I put my slave in your arms, and now that she knows she is pregnant, she despises me. May the Lord judge between you and me." [6]"Your slave is in your hands," Abram said. "Do with her whatever you think best." Then Sarai mistreated Hagar; so she fled from her.

[7]The angel of the Lord found Hagar near a spring in the desert; it was the spring that is beside the road to Shur. [8]And he said, "Hagar, slave of Sarai, where have you come from, and where are you going?" "I'm running away from my mistress Sarai," she answered.

[9]Then the angel of the Lord told her, "Go back to your mistress and submit to her." [10]The angel added, "I will increase your descendants so much that they will be too numerous to count." [11]The angel of the Lord also said to her: "You are now pregnant and you will give birth to a son. You shall name him Ishmael, for the Lord has heard of your misery. [12]He will be a wild donkey of a man; his hand will be against everyone and everyone's hand against him, and he will live in hostility toward all his brothers."

[13]She gave this name to the Lord who spoke to her: "You are the God who sees me," for she said, "I have now seen the One who sees me." [14]That is why the well was called Beer Lahai Roi; it is still there, between Kadesh and Bered. [15]So Hagar bore Abram a son, and Abram gave the name Ishmael to the son she had borne.

Qur'an, Maryam, The Chapter of Mary 19:16–26

[16]And mention in the Book Mary, when she withdrew from her family to an easterly place. [17]Thus did she seclude herself from them, whereupon We sent to her Our Spirit and he became incarnate for her as a perfect human. [18]She said, 'I seek the protection of the All-beneficent from you, should you be Godwary!'

[19]He said, 'I am only a messenger of your Lord that I may give you a pure son.'

[20]She said, 'How shall I have a child seeing that no human being has ever touched me, nor have I been unchaste?'

[21]He said, 'So shall it be. Your Lord says, "It is simple for Me, and so that We may make him a sign for mankind and mercy from Us, and it is a matter [already] decided."'

[22]Thus she conceived him, then withdrew with him to a distant place.

[23]The birth pangs brought her to the trunk of a date palm. She said, 'I wish I had died before this and become a forgotten thing, beyond recall.'

[24]Thereupon he called from below her, [saying,] 'Do not grieve! Your Lord has made a spring to flow at your feet. [25]Shake the trunk of the palm tree, freshly picked dates will drop upon you. [26]Eat, drink and be comforted. Then if you see any human, say, "I have indeed vowed a fast to the All-beneficent, so I will not speak to any human today."'

Qur'an, Al-Qasas, The Chapter of the Stories 28:23–25

23 When [Moses] arrived at the well of Midian, he found there a throng of people watering [their flocks] and he found, besides them, two women holding back [their flock]. He said, 'What is your business?' They said, 'We do not water [our flock] until the shepherds have driven out [their flocks] and our father is an aged man.'

24 So he watered [their flock] for them. Then he withdrew toward the shade and said, 'My Lord! I am indeed in need of any good You may send down to me!'

25 Then one of the two women approached him, walking bashfully. She said, 'My father invites you to pay you the wages for watering [our flock] for us.' So when he came to him and recounted the story to him, he said, 'Do not be afraid. You have been delivered from the wrongdoing lot.' 26 One of the two women said, 'Father, hire him. The best you can indeed hire is a powerful and trustworthy man.'

Bible, John 4:3–15

³ So [Jesus] left Judea and went back once more to Galilee. ⁴ Now he had to go through Samaria. ⁵ So he came to a town in Samaria called Sychar, near the plot of ground Jacob had given to his son Joseph. ⁶ Jacob's well was there, and Jesus, tired as he was from the journey, sat down by the well. It was about noon. ⁷ When a Samaritan woman came to draw water, Jesus said to her, 'Will you give me a drink?' ⁸ (His disciples had gone into the town to buy food.) ⁹ The Samaritan woman said to him, 'You are a Jew and I am a Samaritan woman. How can you ask me for a drink?' (For Jews do not associate with Samaritans.)

¹⁰ Jesus answered her, 'If you knew the gift of God and who it is that asks you for a drink, you would have asked him and he would have given you living water.' ¹¹ 'Sir,' the woman said, 'you have nothing to draw with and the well is deep. Where can you get this living water? ¹² Are you greater than our father Jacob, who gave us the well and drank from it himself, as did also his sons and his livestock?'

¹³ Jesus answered, 'Everyone who drinks this water will be thirsty again, ¹⁴ but whoever drinks the water I give them will never thirst. Indeed, the water I give them will become in them a spring of water welling up to eternal life.' ¹⁵ The woman said to him, 'Sir, give me this water so that I won't get thirsty and have to keep coming here to draw water.' ¹⁶ He told her, 'Go, call your husband and come back.' ¹⁷ 'I have no husband,' she replied. Jesus said to her, 'You are right when you say you have no husband. ¹⁸ The fact is, you have had five husbands, and the man you now have is not your husband. What you have just said is quite true.'

¹⁹ 'Sir,' the woman said, 'I can see that you are a prophet. ²⁰ Our ancestors worshipped on this mountain, but you Jews claim that the place where we must worship is in Jerusalem.'

²¹ 'Woman,' Jesus replied, 'believe me, a time is coming when you will worship the Father neither on this mountain nor in Jerusalem. ²² You Samaritans worship what you do not know; we worship what we do know, for salvation is from the Jews. ²³ Yet a time is coming and has now come when the true worshippers will worship the Father in the Spirit and in truth, for they are the kind of worshippers the Father seeks. ²⁴ God is spirit, and his worshippers must worship in spirit and in truth.' ²⁵ The woman said, 'I know that Messiah' (called Christ) 'is coming. When he comes, he will explain everything to us.' ²⁶ Then Jesus declared, 'I, the one speaking to you – I am he.'

[..]

²⁸ Then, leaving her water jar, the woman went back to the town and said to the people, ²⁹ 'Come, see a man who told me everything I've ever done. Could this be the Messiah?' ³⁰ They came out of the town and made their way towards him. [..] ³⁹ Many of the Samaritans from that town believed in him because of the woman's testimony, 'He told me everything I've ever done.' ⁴⁰ So when the Samaritans came to him, they urged him to stay with them, and he stayed two days. ⁴¹ And because of his words many more became believers.

⁴² They said to the woman, 'We no longer believe just because of what you said; now we have heard for ourselves, and we know that this man really is the Saviour of the world.'

Flower

I love 'simple', and am passionate about the
environment and God's creation.

Lizzie George

Fish

I must admit I picked the fish because it's a great shape for quilling the first time. I do love the sea and my happiest memories are with my family making sandcastles on the beach. I love God's creation and feel really connected to Him walking in nature either under the trees or walking along cliff paths. That feeling of connection is important to me because it's my time for reflecting and talking with Him; when I can use all my senses to feel His awesomeness.

Lizzie George

Oceans

I do miss the water and being by the sea.
Water makes me happy: the beach, the sea,
the reflection of the sun; my happy place.

I made this wave as I listened to 'Oceans'
by Hillsong.

'And I will call upon Your name
And keep my eyes above the waves
When oceans rise
My soul will rest in Your embrace
For I am Yours
You are mine.'

Lauren Worsley

Oceans Rise

'Oceans' has been an anthem to my life for years. Through struggles it has reminded me that I am not alone. God knows what I am going through and He is there with me, holding me up when in life I felt like I was drowning. Now the waves feel smaller and more bearable.

It's been suggested that waves are like opportunities. Life is constantly moving and we can choose to surf those waves and make the most of opportunities. The waves no longer bring the risk of drowning, but of positivity.

Lauren Worsley

The Water of Life

This piece represents the way plants are dependent on water in all four seasons. It also brings to mind God the Creator who made and sustains all things, and Jesus who promised us 'Living Water' to refresh our souls.

Judy Strawson

Holy Well / Calvary

In many countries, sources of water such as springs are valued for their provision of safe, clean water. Some are marked with a cross because they have become places of pilgrimage, revered by Christians. When I looked at this again, I realised it could also represent Calvary and the many blessings that flow from Jesus' death and resurrection.

Judy Strawson

Hagar's Tear

Hagar's Tear represents her suffering and the God who sees and hears her.

Diane Stockwell

Life-Giving Water

Life-Giving Water continues the cycle of nature (and quenches our physical and spiritual thirst).

Diane Stockwell

Fresh Spring

As the rain and the snow
come down from heaven,
and do not return to it
without watering the earth
and making it bud and flourish,
so that it yields seed for the sower and bread
for the eater,
so is my word that goes out from my mouth:
It will not return to me empty,
but will accomplish what I desire
and achieve the purpose for which I sent it.

[Isaiah 55.10-11 Bible]

Sarah Dilworth

Blue Drop

Big Blue Drop
Life goes Flip Flop
Joys coming non-stop
Soaking up pain like a Mop
Angel with every drop
Rewards from an Open Shop
Allah's Mercy Non-Stop
Big Blue Drop

Zaheera Nanabawa

God Knows Us Each by Name

I chose to create an artwork involving the letter C as it is my initial. I believe that God knows each of us by name and everything about us. I know this through the ways He shows His love for me, for example when my prayers are answered and when I spend time talking to and worshipping Him. This helps me to have confidence that God will always be by my side through everything and knows how to help.

I really enjoyed the quilling, especially as it was something I had not tried before, but is now something I would love to do again.

Chloe Worsley

Wherever God Plants You, Bloom with Grace

Allow God to water you,
so your roots are nourished to grow down
deep into his love,
so you blossom,
and become the beautifully formed unique
flower you were always meant to be.

Lisa-Marie Dakin

Two Seas Meeting

The water flows side by side yet the power of the creator never allows them to mix.

"We released the two seas meeting (side by side) : between them a barrier (so) neither of them transgress. Which of the favours of your lord will you deny?"

[Quran 55:19-21]

Fazeela Patel

Tears

A teardrop, so minute in detail but holds the most valuable stories. In it are memories, heartbreak, happiness and love. One will never know until the owner reveals their hidden thoughts.

Fazeela Patel

Women at the Well
Rahima Kholwadia

What I see is someone who is resilient and strong, who can rule the world with her actions. She's not simply fetching water but is silently showing her own strength and value. The drops of water are a sign of freedom and joy.

Life, Water
Rahima Kholwadia

Water is life. Water is a survival instinct. A universe surrounded by water.

Butterfly

At first I thought with the quilling, can I do that? But after I watched the instruction videos, I couldn't stop. I sat every evening doing different colours. Afterwards, I couldn't believe I'd done it!

The thing about water, my mum used to carry those pots on her head. There were six siblings. How much water they would have needed in those pots! You had to kneel down to get them on your head.

I always think water is precious.

Amena Mayat

Ma'an the Water

The Story of Zamzam Well: This "Well" keeps providing water miraculously and strangely, as this valley has no underground source of water. It is definitely the miracle of Allah who brings out water from the barren land, and the well never dries up even after 1400 years. The 'well of Zamzam' is self-replenishing and no one can do this except the Supreme Creator of this whole world, and King of all Kingdoms. May Allah SWT give every Muslim a chance to visit His holy land and a chance to drink this sacred water, as this is the best water in the world. It has been narrated that the Messenger of Allah said, "The best water on the face of the earth is Zamzam water. In it is food for nourishment and healing or cure for illness."

Amena Mayat

Living in His Living Waters

Jesus reached out to the Samaritan woman at the well. He told her He knew all her sins, yet He still loved her. He told her His living water was for everyone including her to start a new life in living hope.
John 4.

As Christians we are followers of Jesus. We are His fishermen. Many Christians wear a fish symbol to show others, their commitment to follow him. I've hidden a fish symbol in this piece.
Mark 1.

Anthea M Searle

Chosen by Him

The story of Hagar in the Bible is not pleasant to read. Hagar is treated without respect or dignity. Yet when she runs away to the wilderness, God sends an Angel to speak with her. Hagar is God's special child and he wants her to focus on her future. He has chosen her.

When she returns from the wilderness, God tells her He won't return her defenceless or with the same status. She will return with strong promises received directly and personally from Him.
Genesis 16.

Anthea M Searle

He Sees Her

The quill on the far right represents the Samaritan woman at the well, in John 4, or Hagar (with baby-quill inside of her) in Genesis 16. She might be thinking that 'the grass is greener on the other side', where all the other women (represented by quills on the left) are gathered together around their well. But she is where God is (represented by the eye) - the One who sees her, and provides water for her - so she is in the best place for herself.

Sometimes we too might wish to be somewhere else, or someone else, but what's more important is whether we can trust in our God who sees us.

Henrietta Cozens

Joy From the Deep

The dolphin is one of God's creatures that leaps for joy after being immersed in the water.

Once we have immersed ourselves in God's living water, Jesus, we too often receive joy.

Henrietta Cozens

Angel Wing, Hagar's Well

When Angel Gabriel touched the heel of Ishmael, a well/spring of rushing water emerged. A powerful force: God's messenger gives earth-rushing water, contained by Hagar into the still water of a well.

Sue Holbrook

Water Cycle

This shows the inter-connectedness of earth/water/plants, which are in an ongoing relationship.

After our first session's 'warm-up' introductions, I discovered Susan (my name) means 'fragrant grass' in Arabic.

Sue Holbrook

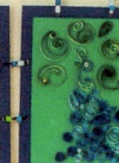

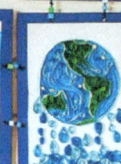

A Reflection on Our Craft

After months of lockdown, in January 2021 Henrietta approached me about getting involved in the craft side of a community project with potentially Muslim and Christian women. As someone else said in our group, referring to the concept of multi-faith women coming together, *"When does this chance come up?.. I don't care what it's about, I'm doing it!"* Those were exactly my thoughts; I was certainly interested.

Quilling, with its flowing fluidity, seemed to fit with the theme of water, coming out of Rana's work on water conservation in Jordan and the 'women at the well' texts that had been set. In quilling, small individual quills are made and then worked together or arranged to make a whole. This seemed to fit with the idea of lots of drops of water making a whole, a puddle, a river or even the sea. We too, as a community of women would be like individual drops ourselves. And we too, would each be producing our own unique quilling piece (drop) which would then be joined up with the others to create a whole.

Linking the pieces with treasury tags would allow the pieces to feel joined but separate, fixed but fluid; one piece of work but with the ability to change its shape, and to have the potential for further pieces to be added.

As we quilled and chatted virtually on Zoom and WhatsApp, our conversations also seemed to take on this fluidity. One thought seemed to lead to another, ideas rippled out and developed. One posted picture set off a flurry of others.

It has been an amazing privilege to be part of this group and to sit back and watch the creativity flow out of and around the group. And then, to see what has been born out of this.

I always love the idea of crafts being accessible and achievable to all. Quilling can be simple. You can buy special quilling paper and equipment, but you don't have to. You can, and we did, create something very beautiful with plain paper and a cocktail stick. Why don't you have a go?!

Edi Wilson
Craft Facilitator

You can quill too! Basic quilling with basic tools.

1.

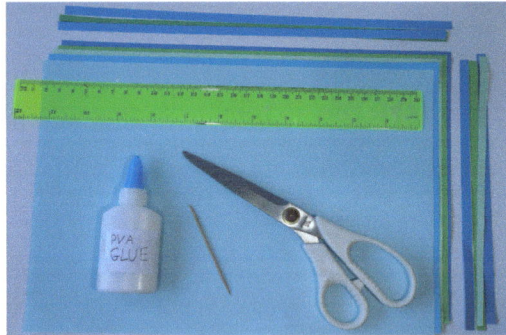

You need paper, PVA glue and a cocktail stick. We used A4 copy paper. Paper weight 80-120 gsm is good but most paper works. Cut straight strips of paper about 3mm-8mm wide. These are your *quilling strips*.

2.

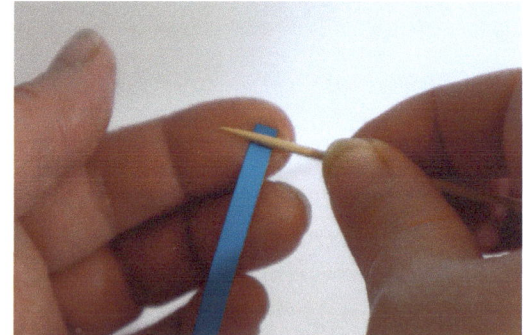

Hold the cocktail stick between your right thumb and right index finger. Place the end of a quill strip on your left index finger. Press the cocktail stick firmly onto the quilling strip.

3.

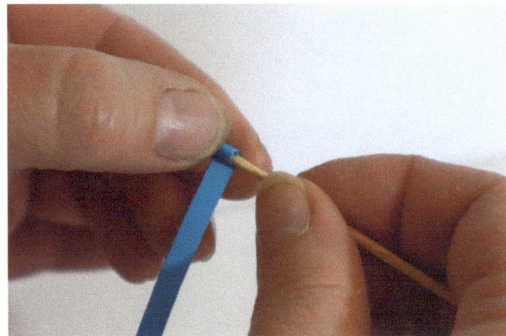

Use your left thumb to start rolling the quilling strip. The thumb needs to move downwards repeatedly. Roll the quill strip to the end. You are now *quilling*, making a *quill*.

4.

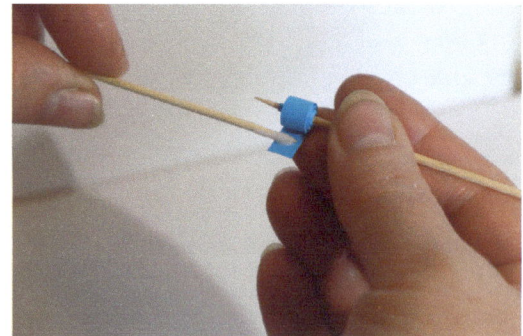

While the quilling strip is still on the cocktail stick, stick the end down with a very small amount of glue. When gluing hold firmly for ten seconds. The paper will stick better with less glue.

5.

Take the coil off the cocktail stick.
This is a *tight coil*.

6.

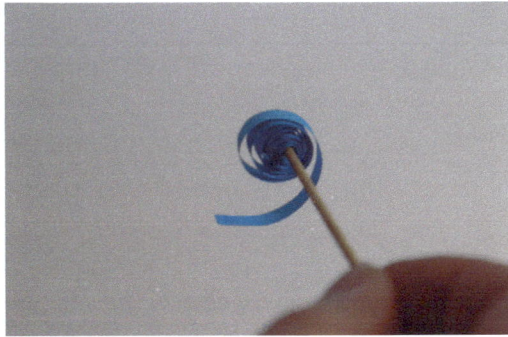

To make a loose coil follow steps 2 & 3. Before the gluing step,
release the paper quill and let it unroll loosely.

7.

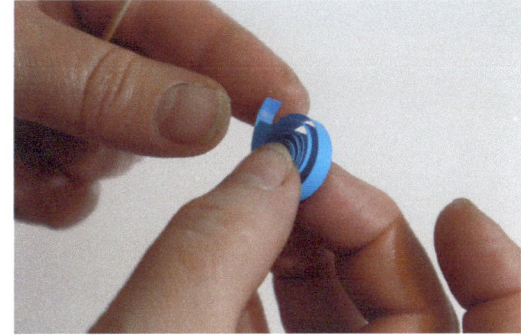

Stick the end down to make a loose coil.

8.

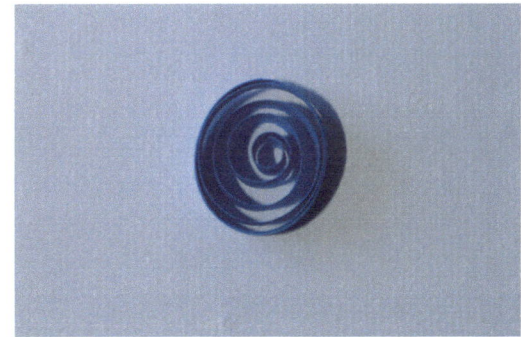

This is a *loose coil.*

9.

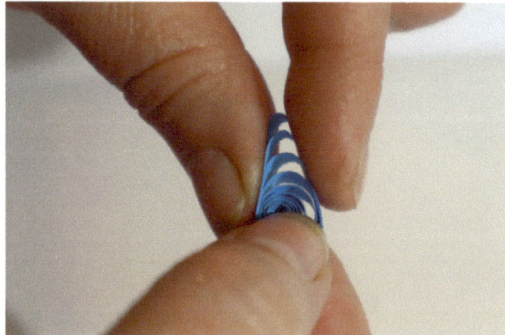

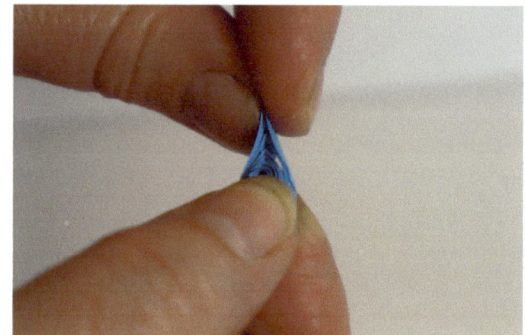

To make a *tear drop* first make a loose coil by following steps 2, 3, 6 & 7.
Hold the loose coil in your right hand and use your left hand to lightly pull up the coil and pinch one end of it into the shape you want.

10.

This is your *tear drop quill*.

11.

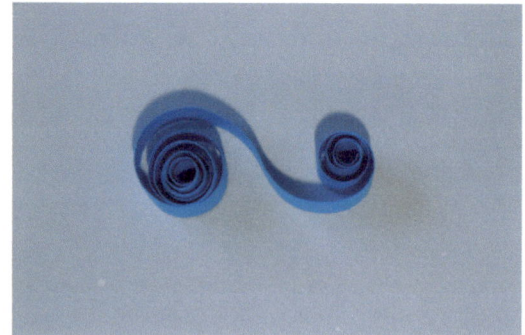

To make a *scroll quill* start steps 2 & 3 on one end of your quilling strip. Stop quilling when you get halfway. Quill the other end of the quilling strip too.

12.

To make a *swirl*, hold three quilling strips together and fold them in half.

13.

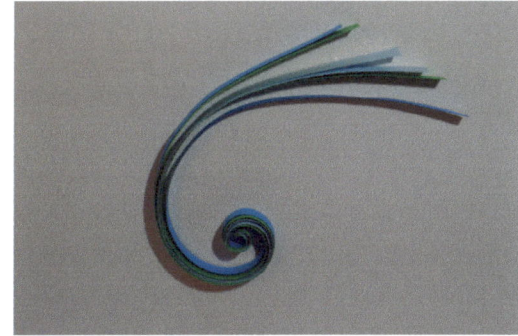

Holding the three quilling strips together, start to quill from the folded ends as far as you want.

14.

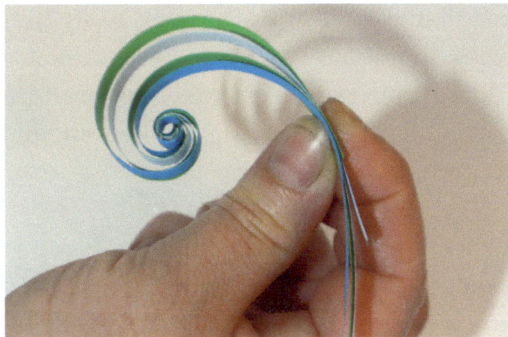

Use your fingers to gently slide the quilling strips apart to make the swirl shape. Glue the quilling strips together where the fingers are pinching to hold in place.

15.

You can cut off the ends or quill the ends of the swirls to add more decoration.

Have Fun Quilling!

A Reflection on Water Around the World

Consider...

To find water in the UK, you only have to turn a tap. There is water available 24 hours a day, seven days a week. In contrast in Jordan, with a population of 10 million people including 1.5 million Syrian refugees, most people collect rainwater on their roofs, and have running water for just 24 hours a week.

300 mm (30 cm) of rain falls a year in Jordan, whereas the average annual rainfall in the UK is 900 mm (90 cm). Out of 12 groundwater basins in Jordan, 10 are being pumped below deficit.

80 litres/person/day is the average use of water in Jordan, while in the UK it is 145 litres.

The internationally accepted threshold level for access to safe water is 20 litres per person per day. That equals about three toilet flushes.

According to the World Wildlife Fund, in South Africa it takes 860 litres of water to produce a 500-gram steak. This is the equivalent of 13 showers. The Anglican Church of South Africa, a church of 3-4 million people, has declared a climate emergency and is scaling up its use of renewable energy.

Nearly ⅙ of the world's population (1.1 billion people) do not have access to clean drinking water, and most of these live on less than 5 litres of water a day. More than a third of earth's citizens do not have access to basic sanitation. Many rely on dirty water from open rivers, lakes and wells, or spend several hours collecting water every day. Others spend large parts of their restricted income to buy water.

Water conservation is number 6 on the UN Sustainability Goals.

Christians and Muslims are working together in Jordan to conserve water. Dr Rana Abu-Maines is researching their efforts and presented the above facts (and the quotation on the right) to the Women at the Well group in 2021.

A message attributed to an unnamed Hopi elder of Arizona, one of the USA's First Nations:

"You have been telling the people that this is the Eleventh Hour, now you must go and tell the people that this is the Hour. And there are things that need to be considered:

Where are you living?
What are you doing?
What are your relationships?
Are you in right relation?
Where is your water?
Know your garden.

It is time to speak your Truth.
Create your community.
Be good to each other."

Then he clasped his hands together, smiled, and said,

"This could be a good time! There is a river flowing now very fast. It is so great and swift that there are those who will be afraid. They will try to hold on to the shore. They will feel they are torn apart and will suffer greatly. Know the river has its destination. The elders say we must let go of the shore, push off into the middle of the river, keep our eyes open, and our heads above water. And I say, see who is in there with you and celebrate...

The time for the lone wolf is over. Gather yourselves! All that we do now must be done in a sacred manner and in celebration. We are the ones we've been waiting for."

Water is a gift.

Reduce - Reuse - Recycle - Rejoice!